ALSO AVAILABLE

MASTERS AT WORK

BECOMING A FASHION DESIGNER

LINDSAY PEOPLES WAGNER

SIMON & SCHUSTER

New York   London   Toronto   Sydney   New Delhi

Simon & Schuster
1230 Avenue of the Americas
New York, NY 10020

First Simon & Schuster hardcover edition September 2019

SIMON & SCHUSTER and colophon are registered trademarks of
Simon & Schuster, Inc.

For information about special discounts for bulk purchases,
please contact Simon & Schuster Special Sales at 1-866-506-1949 or
business@simonandschuster.com.

The Simon & Schuster Speakers Bureau can bring authors to
your live event. For more information or to book an event, contact
the Simon & Schuster Speakers Bureau at 1-866-248-3049 or
visit our website at www.simonspeakers.com.

Manufactured in the United States of America

1   3   5   7   9   10   8   6   4   2

Library of Congress Cataloging-in-Publication Data has been applied for.

ISBN 978-1-9821-2113-6
ISBN 978-1-9821-2114-3 (ebook)

CONTENTS

BECOMING A
FASHION DESIGNER

INTRODUCTION

S ay something. I've found myself repeating those two words over and over again throughout my life in fashion. I've said them while waiting for emerging designers' first shows to start. I've said them clicking through look books that all look like Celine or Gucci knockoffs. I've said them watching the most expensive and elaborate shows with the most boring clothes. There is a lot of noise and glamour in the fashion industry. There is also a healthy amount of nepotism, politics, who's who, and who you know. While those things endure, the one thing that remains is a need for someone to say something. What really matters is for a designer to communicate something so authentic and real that it breaks through in a visceral way.

Creating clothing that transcends time or preconceived notions—that's what being a fashion designer is about. There's a lot that goes into saying something. It starts with where you come from creatively, how you developed your vision, and what you want people to feel when they see your brand. The designers who break through inject clothing with meaning. They speak even to those who don't particularly care, all the while reflecting and creating the zeitgeist.

If you do a quick Google search or walk into a bookstore, you'll find very few books on how to be a fashion designer—and for good reason. There's no universal template. No one can give you the pencil and paper to start, no one can interpret your perspective, and there is no get-rich-quick guide. You can go to Central Saint Martins or Parsons School of Design, train under the right people, know the right editors, have endless funding, make interesting collections, and still falter. Even if you "do everything right," there is still no guarantee, and what it means to be a fashion designer now is starkly different than what it meant twenty years ago, or even five years go. The groundbreaking designer Virgil Abloh, who founded his own haute streetwear brand Off-White and works as the men's artistic director of Louis Vuitton, admitted, "I'd sort of agree I'm not a designer; this term seems like it's for traditionalists," he says. "TBD the new title."

People think of the fashion industry as this frivolous, carefree environment where everyone is twirling around in sequins, drinking champagne. On the surface sometimes that assumption can be right, but those who have made a real impact on the industry know all too well that it takes an unprecedented level of focus to have longevity and be more than a blip of hype on Instagram. They know the work, have done the work, and continue to do the work. Those who are resilient and have persevered, like Christopher John Rogers of his self-named label, Becca McCharen-Tran of Chromat, and Rosie Assoulin of her eponymous brand, can tell you all that's left is an innate desire to offer something that's unfiltered, consuming, and dynamic.

I am currently the youngest and only Black editor in chief in the United States at a major publication. My perspective about what it means to be a designer is different from people who have been in the fashion industry for forty years. Though there may never be another Karl Lagerfeld or Ralph Lauren, the industry has opened itself up to so much fresh talent. It is an exciting time to be a designer. New designers constantly bring something fresh to the table that we've never seen before. I've seen the good and the bad, the original and the unoriginal, and enough to know the difference. Working my way up the ranks, first as fashion market editor at Style.com, then at *New York* magazine's fashion blog *The Cut*, and now as editor in chief of *Teen Vogue*, has shaped my worldview of what it means to influence the design world no matter what is currently trendy or cool.

I talk to a lot of young designers in the early stages of their careers. People come up to me on the street or after I've spoken on a panel and ask how to be seen in this industry. With this book I hope to give guidance and advice to any person invested in making fashion design their life's work.

First of all, there is no easy way in, and there's no easy way to stay in. Every part of my career has been me clawing up a hill, hoping that my creativity, originality, and pure grit to outwork others will prove to be useful. If you're wondering whether you're in the right field, what it entails to be a designer, or how much money you would need to start your own collection, use this unfiltered book as a starting point to think about your future. When I began working in fashion I felt bitter because I read every magazine from cover to cover, but those publications never explained how long I would need to intern, that I would make nine dollars an hour as an assistant, and that I was expected to wear head-to-toe designer clothing every single day. The realities of working in the industry continue to shock me, whether it's the hours, the politics, or the economics. I made it work in my early days: I changed mannequins at the DKNY store during weeknights, on the weekends waited tables at a restaurant, and took any freelance gigs I could with stylists in my spare time. I decided to write this book because I wish something similar had been available when I started. It would have been immensely helpful to know what I was getting into before I left the Midwest for New York to embark on this path.

To show you how it's really done, what becoming a fashion designer really entails today, I followed three distinct designers. Each one has found their own way to stand out despite the noise, and established themselves as undeniable presences in the rapidly changing landscape of fashion. Learning from their experiences, this book tells the broader story of a career as a fashion designer.

I chose to talk with Christopher John, Becca, and Rosie because they have been influential in my career in fashion and because they are so open about their own pressures, successes, failures, and everything in between. I love their work—and I firmly believe they've made a permanent mark not only on the insular space of fashion but also on the world.

There are hundreds of thousands of designers. The vast majority work at major fashion houses, but these three people had the courage to start their own enterprises, which are turning into midsize companies with recognizable names in different sectors and with different goals for their brands.

It's one thing to be included in reviews for fashion shows, but it's another for a generation of young people to feel connected to your brand as if they know the inner workings of your soul. These brands represent a new breed of pioneering fashion voices who have created a bond with their consumers in an organic way. To show the breadth of what it takes to be a designer, I chose three designers at different stages of their careers. Starting in 2012, Christopher John Rogers founded his eponymous brand, Becca McCharen-Tran of Chromat has been building her brand for nearly ten years, and Rosie Assoulin, whose design background began when she was fourteen, is working tirelessly to grow her already established brand bigger than she ever thought possible. Each designer demonstrates the story of each phase of a fashion designer's journey. It's never the same, nothing is concrete, but there is a universality you will find within the experiences of these bold, independent creators.

All three of these designers are also vital to the industry because they are leading the conversation on a trend before it happens. Making clothing that speaks to a generation seems almost too daunting to even grasp, but it's something they have been able to do at different points of their careers because they understand that style is something to be taken seriously. It has to speak to people on a personal, emotional, and psychological level.

Once a designer's worldview has been established, it still takes an eye that's willing to be developed over time. Fashion rarely sleeps, and with the prominence of fast fashion, the cycle of trends is ever evolving. The fact is that the world has changed, and the internet and social media have remade the fashion industry in ways never thought possible. For decades it had been all about being exclusive and selling an aspirational dream, but now essentially anyone on social media can say they are a designer and maybe even get the attention of magazine editors and retail buyers. And, more than ever, designers are quick to follow a trend that's popular on social media to get in on some of that capital for their own brand instead of taking a beat and finding their own lane and internal inspiration. It's one thing to be inspired because people are into a specific trend or look at a certain time. It's another to appropriate an idea from a culture to make it mainstream but not include that culture in the models on the runway or in the campaign or with the people you hire to make your brand succeed. We've seen countless brands get scolded for stealing designs thanks to people behind the Instagram account Diet Prada, and on the other side we've seen a lot of independent designers get burned by major fast-fashion retailers like Zara and H&M without getting credit. All of this has really split fashion design into two territories—designers who lead and designers who react. After all, every single design is in conversation with other work that has come before it, constantly mutating and evolving. Even the consumer has drastically changed. We are now living in a time when an audience or customer is able to communicate directly with a brand, saying they don't like a design. Consumers are fickle and move on from a trend quicker than it took for it to emerge. Younger consumers are much more vocal about social and environmental issues, and they want transparency about point of view, how things are made, and what you stand for. All these issues directly affect the bottom dollar. Campaigns on everything from gun control to racial and gender equality like #BlackLivesMatter, #MeToo, and #TimesUp are critical for brands if they want to get the attention of the all powerful Generation Z and millennial consumers who represent $350 billion spending power in the United States alone.

Business of Fashion and McKinsey & Company's *The State of Fashion 2019* showed that the top three words to describe the fashion industry are: *changing*, *digital*, and *fast*. So, for a designer today, there has to be the perfect storm culmination of talent, influence, and message. Designers now have to represent the brand in a front-facing way, and often have to find a way to produce multiple revenue streams. Founder and designer of JW Anderson and creative director of Loewe Jonathan Anderson once said, "We have this perceived illusion of what the fashion designer does. As an industry, we make it out that this one individual changes the entire face of the earth. I have never said 'me'; it's always 'we.' I am just the big salesman."

And while you may be fortunate enough to start a brand and never interact with consumers, more often than not being the face and allowing people to see your own humanity is what is going to bring you consumers in this age of transparency. There's also the reality of so many positions in fashion being condensed, with editors working at multiple brands instead of one, or covering all the market instead of just being a swimsuit editor who solely attends Miami Swim week shows and doesn't bother with any of the clothing markets. The same goes in the design world, because running a full traditional atelier doesn't financially make sense for most designers anymore, so being the face—and also the behind-the-scenes merchandiser, technician, and whatever is needed—is imperative.

So, what does this all mean for the future of fashion design? A lot more than it used to. Designer Marc Jacobs famously said, "Clothes mean nothing until someone lives in them." The reality is that there are countless designers all over the world, but getting someone to choose *your* brand time and time again is what makes it all come alive. The instant language that fashion has become, representing what you stand for and whom you align yourself with has moved fashion designers from sitting in their own ivory towers to a place where connectivity and cultural expression are the most valuable tools. Getting to the bottom of what you want to communicate with your clothing is what most designers realize too late. If you are saying that you want people to have a certain flair and attitude, it has to evoke that in every stitch.

If you want people to feel like the elevated, better version of themselves, communicate what that means in the tailoring and ease of the design. If you want to reinvent what is aspirational and over-the-top, communicate your wildest dreams that will make people want to be part of them. I don't believe it's a designer's job to make clothing for everyone, but there has to be someone in mind—someone just fabulous enough to pull it off, someone waiting to blossom in what you have made. You can make beautiful clothing that looks like art, but if no one is wearing or buying it, then you don't have a business. So if you're telling a story that's already been told, don't be surprised if no one is inspired to buy it. Telling a story that's never been told, one that's solely yours to tell, is what a designer is in today's society.

Brands that are beholden to old-school business models (e.g., doing shows every season) and stuck in outdated traditions (e.g., creating garments solely for red-carpet moments) end up locked in a downward spiral of spending too much without a return in capital or engaged customers. Traditionalists in the fashion industry maintain that you have to have a certain pedigree and credentials to be in the trade and flourish, but the new wave of designers unapologetically come from all walks of life, proudly bringing their opinions to center stage. Being decisive about what you stand for will sustain you much longer in the industry than any fancy education will. Becoming a fashion designer requires a great deal of reflection, awareness, and balancing of the practical and possible. Designers must take people out of their lives, to a different place and mind-set.

What you choose to put on the runway, show at a presentation, put in a look book, or post on Instagram matters because it can change someone's mind. Yes, the business-minded designers behind brands like Christopher John Rogers, Chromat, and Rosie Assoulin have figured out the details of how much money they need and how to make it last, they have navigated how to stay true to themselves even when things didn't sell, but above all else they've made the banal exciting, and that's what it takes to shape the culture.

One thing I instantly noticed about Christopher John Rogers when I met him is that, unlike other young designers, he is the least concerned about superficial "likes" and is smart enough to know that popularity doesn't make up for a lack of talent or good, old-fashioned work ethic. His aesthetic is very much his own, bringing together his Southern, Baton Rouge, Louisiana, roots and life in New York as a black man. A purist in every way, he cares about the craftsmanship of everything—from his signature voluminous and ruffled dresses to the shapes and less-explored silhouettes in his new collection—and takes pride in the things most people think are too small to care about. There's a certain finesse in every decision. Everything he creates challenges the idea of what modern women's everyday clothing could be, balancing the drama with the everyday. When I think about a standout emerging designer from the past five years, Rogers first comes to mind because buying his clothing and following his journey on social media is like reading the diary of someone great before everyone knows it.

While reviewing the transcript from my interview with Rogers, there's a certain ease and confidence in his voice that you don't find in most emerging designers. He starts out by saying, "I want younger people to know that you can just embrace all of the specific nuances of the things that you like, and that will make your voice singular and complete." There's so much wisdom and knowledge in his background and references, but there's also the realization that the best thing he has going for himself is his own identity. And in a sea of designers who struggle to find their niche, Rogers has succeeded and become even less afraid of telling his personal story through his designs. He is still just as hungry was when he graduated from school (if not more so), focusing on digging deep within himself to find out what he wants to communicate and how he wants to feel.

That conversation led me to Becca McCharen-Tran of Chromat, who has been in the business almost ten years. Her progressive swimwear and bodywear designs are fun and futuristic—and welcome you just as you are. McCharen-Tran was one of the first designers to take size inclusivity seriously, especially in an area (beachwear) that has for so long excluded women who aren't sample size. Ever since its inception, Chromat has been known for its inclusive casting, using models that are diverse in size, ability, race, and gender. The people who walk in Chromat runway shows and are cast in its campaigns have bodies that have traditionally been excluded from them. Yet McCharen-Tran feels that it's innately important to her as a brand and human being to incorporate everyone. That consideration has been vital to her business and the greater good of the fashion industry since there are only a handful of designers who take representation as seriously as McCharen-Tran does.

Everything she makes is playful, most likely neon and

bright, but the designs are incredibly technical. Drawstrings were added a few seasons ago to most pieces since they provide a personalized fit for a range of body types, fabrics are all sourced from materials that are durable and don't add waste to the environment, and there are regular fit tests to make sure that the size 4X swimsuit fits as well as the size small. Her most recent collection, designed in Miami, reflecting the dangers of climate change, since global warming and rising sea levels could one day very soon bring the reality of swimwear as everyday attire no matter where you live.

McCharen-Tran then led me to Rosie Assoulin, a creative ahead of her time whose aim is to give working women something beautiful and dramatic to make the weight of the world feel more bearable. Every piece has a bit of romance and flair yet is practical enough to throw on for a regular day. That's an incredibly hard line to tow. You know a Rosie piece because it's easy to wear, detailed, and has an element of surprise that makes it stand out. While she previously worked at Oscar de la Renta and Lanvin and won the CFDA Swarovski Award for Womenswear a year after launching her eponymous label, the most impressive thing about Assoulin is her ability to make everything a wearable piece of art.

Her collections incorporate bold colors and patterns. There is deep thought behind what fabric would be the most voluminous. Add a touch of effortless glamour and some small details that add a dash of humor. Even simpler pieces like a blazer are never just a blazer with Assoulin. She pushes the boundaries of contemporary suiting with not a single boring black blazer in sight. Instead it's bright-blue corduroy with oversized lapels and a nipped waist.

Yes, most people in fashion start out animating their ideas after picking up magazines or following certain designers and trends. Rogers, McCharen-Tran, and Assoulin all did. But making a tangible piece out of imagery and experience is dependent upon an ability to create. All three designers have radically different viewpoints and are at very different stages in their careers. What unites them is an understanding that their mission as designers is about far more than clothes. It is essential to everyday life. Delving into the stories of these three people is my way of opening the pipeline so that young designers can have a chance and know the tools they need to be part of the fashion industry.

The first step is starting with the groundwork. The learned skills that are the bedrock of what it takes to turn sketches into clothing and into a successful business and brand. There are so many creatives who are left out of the conversation because of a lack of planning, resources, connections, and transparency as to what it would take to get their lines started. A good friend once told me that working in fashion is like building a house, and building a fashion brand is exactly like that. You can constantly be working on smaller things, and it feels like nothing is getting done, but with the right materials, funding, and team, you start to see something appear before your eyes. It won't happen overnight, but in the end, hopefully you've built a house that passionately says something to the world that you can call your own.

1

GROUNDWORK

To lay the foundation of a career in fashion design, I'll start from the ground up. In writing this book, I did not want to assume any privilege, or background, in the field, so if you know absolutely nothing about the realities of the business before we get to the stories of the designers, keep reading. This chapter will dive into the million little details behind the scenes that you need to know before you even start. The reality is that the fashion industry has become survival of the fittest.

Even though the industry is growing, more than 95 percent of start-up fashion businesses fail and, more often than not, the ups and downs of trying to get a new fashion business off the ground is enough to make most designers quit. In the years I've been in the industry and after talking with Christopher John Rogers, Becca McCharen-Tran, and Rosie Assoulin, the most important thing to do from the start is ask questions. A lot of them. There can be mystery around where people really get funding from, or what it takes to actually make a dream turn into reality, but fundamentally starting a fashion line is a business. Money comes in and money goes out. Your time will be spent not only designing, but sample trafficking (if you choose to make samples), working on production with suppliers, managing your team, begging for press and editors' attention, and in general just trying to keep the lights on.

I can't tell you how many designers have tried and failed and tried and failed and tried again only to finally learn what it took for them to be successful enough to keep the business going at a steady pace. It's much more complicated than just getting a fashion-design degree and expecting things to fall in place because people have told you you're talented. Creative fields are not linear. Everything is relative to your experience, abilities, connections, and economic stability.

The debate of whether you have to go school to become a designer depends on who you ask. Some of my favorite and most prolific designers in the industry like Miuccia Prada, Karl Lagerfeld, and Manolo Blahnik never went to school, and Michael Kors enrolled at Fashion Institute

of Technology (FIT) but dropped out after nine months and went to go work at Bergdorf Goodman. On the other hand, the experience and connections made at school is often what allows designers to build their brand. School provides a security bubble. It's a chance to incubate without having to be directionless. This decision truly depends on your financial situation and what suits your personality. School can give you the safe space to learn, experiment, get critiques from professionals in the industry, and force you to find your voice, but some also find it stifling and would rather be immersed in their own world to create.

If you are interested in fashion schools, the ones with the best track record as far as graduates and guidance are Central Saint Martins, Parsons, and FIT. There are plenty of second- and third-tier design schools in smaller cities, but if you want to compete against the best then being in a fashion epicenter metropolis like London, Paris, or New York is where you'll either sink or swim. Central Saint Martins in London has the most famous graduates—a casual list includes Alexander McQueen, Stella McCartney, Riccardo Tisci, and Phoebe Philo. It's elite in every way, including the price of tuition, but members of the staff are legends, so they have firsthand knowledge in and out of the classroom. Parsons in New York has guided careers like Marc Jacobs, Tom Ford, and Alexander Wang, and in the past decades the talent coming out of this school has excelled. It's common for past graduates like Jack McCollough and Lazaro Hernandez of Proenza Schouler or Prabal Gurung to host invaluable workshops for students, and tuition. FIT in New York is the most affordable of the three, with graduates like Calvin Klein and Carolina Herrera, but it's also known for its exceptional degrees that allow you to take courses on textiles, fashion business, and marketing. Bigger fashion houses have the budget and infrastructure to hire a lot of people in the textile and business sectors, while independent designers must take on those responsibilities themselves, which is something to consider since there are fewer fashion houses with large budgets. Be prepared to take on those duties if you choose to start your own namesake line.

Taking the initiative to understand the basics of the creative process—sketching, sewing, draping—is something you have learn for yourself. Those are technical trade skills that take focus, time, patience, and practice. Keep in mind that not everyone knows what type of fashion designer they want to be until they try different sectors; sometimes taking classes helps designers figure out which is best for them. The main types of design are apparels and accessories. Apparels is the only sector that breaks down into very divided subcategories: haute couture, ready-to-wear, and mass market. Haute couture is clothing designed with customization at the forefront. Customers are usually very wealthy, frequent clients who expect the brand to customize any piece to their liking, preferences, and exact measurements. Ready-to-wear is the most common and features contemporary designs created for a general market that would ideally be sold off the rack in stores or in your own flagship. Mass market waters down any ideas from haute couture and ready-to-wear into pieces that can be manufactured in enormous quantities at highly affordable prices. So if you had an intricately sequined haute couture ball gown, it would most likely translate into a midi-length dress with less intricately done sequins in ready-to-wear, and mass market would use the cheapest, shiniest sequins available on a shift dress.

Accessories includes a much larger assortment of items, such as shoes, handbags, jewelry, belts, hats, hair accessories, sunglasses, scarves, and wallets. They come at a range of price points but don't really see a divide in the market because people regularly want affordable casual shoes but may also want to invest in a pair of red-soled Louboutins they saw their favorite celebrity wear on the red carpet.

THESE SECTORS CAN OVERLAP, but only once you have achieved status in the market you've chosen. For example, you may be a shoe designer and want to expand to bags since both are technically accessories, but most young shoe designers only find success when they have become a staple in that market and can convince consumers that they need a bag with the same aesthetic to match that pair of shoes, like Mansur Gavriel. Simply put, when starting out, don't take on more than you can handle. Focus on your strengths.

Oftentimes designers have a lot of scattered ideas and cannot hone in on the one message they want to get out that will foster other ideas. Your collection should define who you are as a designer and what you present each season. Establish your name and core collection before you diverse into sublines (i.e., a diffusion line that's more affordable or an athleisure line). Use these beginning stages to define your artistic and creative vision.

Are you aiming to solve a problem or simply create your wildest dreams? Are you inspired by people in fashion around you or desire to create your own universe? Consider starting with a mood board, or collection of images that inspire you to point yourself in the right direction. Immerse yourself in all things visual. Balance your inspiration between the current and timeless so you don't get too consumed by what's happening now. Try things you've never done or even wanted to before. Stepping out of your comfort zone and taking risks in the beginning stages will pay off, even if not immediately. It shows you the possibilities and avenues to evolve into. The bottom line is that the technical, logistical, and financial details of being a fashion designer can be worked out, but creative vision is either there or not.

While that might have seemed like a journey already, just know that there is a lifetime between something being on a mood board and it being sold in stores. The creative process for every designer differs, but the starting point for most is to find inspiration in research. It could be an era in time, a garden, a silhouette, a movie, a musician, a family scrapbook, or anything else. Creating a mood board of what materials, imagery, and aesthetic you want to hone in on can help you decide where you're going. Inspiration can come from looking at iconic designers or going to a vintage store, but it can also come from traveling, looking at art, or what people are wearing on the street. Keep in mind that some designers look into trend forecasting as research for their next collection as to predict what colors and silhouettes will be popular in the upcoming season, or turn to buyers to see what has been selling at luxury department stores. So much of this initial process has to do with personal preference, design capabilities, and budget. Be resourceful, inventive, and curious. Trust your instincts. And don't forget to ask questions.

Once you've found your inspiration for the collection, it's time to start sketching and draping. Most start by sketching by hand or digitally with computer-aided design (CAD) software. Sketching by hand is preferred for most since you can include fluidity to the piece and get a better idea of draping and how the piece will move. CAD helps add dimensionality and allows you to quickly edit and see if what seems like a good idea would actually look good. Some designers aren't naturals at sketching and would rather play with fabrics directly on a dress form. But keep in mind this all depends on your budget and skill level. Textiles are expensive.

The next step is usually cutting, sewing, and fitting the garment. At bigger fashion houses there's an in-house pattern-making team that works with the design team to bring to life all the intricate details that were originally envisioned. So if you're working independently or with a smaller team, be prepared to go back and forth to get from sketch to the muslin, which is the cheap, early version of your garment. This is the part that can really make or break a designer, since it's so tedious to get something you imagine to come to life with the magic you hoped. Be prepared to go through fifty silhouettes, and edit down from there to focus on your strongest pieces to make samples of. Understanding the nuanced differences between certain textiles comes in handy at this point. Cotton acts differently than leather or silk— but it all depends on how you envision the piece and what's the most feasible for production (e.g, your budget and intended consumer). Sacrifices like choosing between cashmere and merino wool, real fur and faux fur, silk chiffon and polyester chiffon are very common.

The goal is for the collection to have a mix of options retail buyers will be interested in for profitability and conceptual pieces for higher-price-point buyers or to be considered for editorial purposes and the red carpet.

Once the patterns are refined and the fits perfected, pieces can go into production and be made in quantities that you prefer and can afford.

The truth is that the process I explained is much more of a tradition now, with designers also being creative heads. It is still widely respected when designers know how to do everything themselves, but it is no longer a requirement. Today, there is much more of a divide between "vanity designers" who hire designers to draw, drape, cut, and sew to make their creations come to life, and traditional designers who do everything themselves. Whether in or out of school or knowing how to make everything yourself or not, understanding fabric on a technical level will make or break your ability to create clothing that makes sense from a design standpoint but also ensures your bottom line. On paper a lot of things can be beautiful, but the basic knowledge of how a fabric reacts when its worn on the runway, how it breathes, and the way it drapes on the body differentiates the amateurs from the pros.

Most emerging designers show their samples to editors and stylists, hoping they'll be shot or featured in publications to help create brand awareness. Buyers are usually overly confident that sales and traffic in the store or online will increase, which will in turn make up a large portion of sales for your brand. Buyers aren't able to put a lot of brands in stores or e-commerce anymore because it requires them to hold inventory stock. Buyers, suppliers, and designers want to make the largest profit, so the number of designers who are approached by editors and buyers is increasingly small.

Most young designers they tell me their dreams are to get their collections seen by editors and buyers who can propel their career to fame and fortune. Then they ask if they should start their own business or work for a major fashion house. In my personal experience, I've had young designers come to my office and say that they're ready to be in Barneys New York windows, and then I am immediately disappointed by the obvious red flags when I review their work. Their collection isn't cohesive or edited, or the quality is lacking. What I would rather see is a hungry designer with a unique, focused aesthetic. Maybe it's not the largest collection, but the pieces have a strong attitude and are made from quality materials. Designers like the latter make me believe there is something magical in their future.

Choosing between starting your own collection or working for someone else is a test of faith and your economic situation. For a lot of young people coming into the industry, it helps to at least have some experience working at a house because you see firsthand how everything in the business and brand functions. Immediately out of school, young designers are so eager to start their own brand without having fully fleshed out what they have to say. So if you're not at that point yet, get experience while you wait.

Most design students get early experience by interning at fashion houses or, once they graduate, by working an entry-level position like a design assistant. You won't get paid much and you'll definitely be overworked. It helps to be passionate about the designer you're working for so you can understand the process start to finish. Depending on what market you're interested in, it can be quite competitive to get a position at a coveted brand like Dior or Chanel. The day-to-day responsibilities may differ, but you'll spend most of your time fitting models to refine pieces, tracking samples and factory production, and analyzing fabrics. It's unlikely that you'll be sketching anything that actually makes it into the collection, but the experience and exposure is priceless.

There's also something to be said for finding your own

people—or a team—who have the same vision as you but different strengths to help get your collection started. Many of the most well-known designers like Marc Jacobs, Alexander McQueen, and Giorgio Armani have been able to excel in the industry due to finding a like-minded business partner. Someone who understood their creative vision but was able to work on the everyday operations of the business. In such a competitive industry, you have to find a way to commercialize your creativity.

So once you have something to say, firm ideas, creative vision, and actualized pieces, you'll need a business plan. A business plan helps sketch out a sustainable financial game plan. It makes sure you won't be a one-hit wonder. Hopefully your business plan will allow you to transition from the few samples you've made to being able to create a legitimate collection that usually has better models, hair, makeup, and photography for look books and social media.

I like to think of this phase less as a boring business plan and more a road map for your brand. So if we are building this house of a fashion brand, this is what a construction crew would do at a building site before they put concrete down to construct the foundation for a house. There's usually a bulldozer involved to clear away debris, move around soil and gravel, and level the ground before anything is even built. The process of making a business plan is brutal, but it gives you a solid base to build on, preventing shaky ground.

It may seem like creative people shouldn't have to do a long and expansive business plan full of numbers and objectives, but that's the exact kind of thinking that has led a lot of talented designers to fail. A lack of foresight and infrastructure can be deadly. Instead of thinking of it as purely about numbers, use it as a tool to be specific about your vision to outline both creative and financial decisions, and as a guide to say where your strengths and weaknesses are. In the early stages of financing your business you could have survived from one piece sold to the next, but in order to have longevity you have to stop living paycheck to paycheck and plan for pieces that do not sell. A creative vision without a plan is lacking thought into the nitty-gritty details. If there is no blueprint for your house it will likely never come to fruition and be built.

To get investors on board, you'll need a clear, focused, and persuasive business plan. Investors not only provide up-front cash and capital but they also will be an invaluable source of counsel and advice on your path forward.

Ideally your investors have deep experience in the fashion industry. They know how to navigate choppy waters and grow business from upstarts to scalable operations. The best ones open doors in more ways than one.

Your business plan should include an executive summary, objectives, market analysis, implementation plan, and financials. The executive summary should clearly describe your vision of why someone should invest in you and your brand. Explain what's niche about your brand and include highlights of what investors should know. It should be concise but not vague. Do not use artsy terms or buzzwords. Who precisely is your customer? Go into detail about who you're designing for, what other brands they're currently buying, where they shop, and how much money they spend on clothing. Talk with friends whom you've made things for and people who have had interest in your collection. Look at retailers to identify a price range that's realistic but also brings in the revenue necessary to expand. A lot of designers in recent years have found that accessories, a staple item, or something at an accessible price point like a logo T-shirt paired with more expensive pieces allow them to see mass market appeal and profits, as well as acclaim. That is a winning combination that looks attractive to investors and provides capital to be able to continue to make creative pieces even if all of them aren't selling. Whether it's Proenza Schouler's tie-dye T-shirts that average under $300, Fendi's bag charms that average $500, or Chanel's jumbo classic flap bag that's currently at $6,200 but increases in price and value every year, the most successful businesses have a core piece that speaks to the DNA of the brand and also helps build revenue.

Next, outline your objectives of what you aim to do with your brand. This will help investors visualize your goals not just for your initial collections but what you'll do five to ten years from now. This will also help make your collections strong and more cohesive once you've narrowed down the who and why. Once you have made it clear who you are, where you are going, and why people will not be able to ignore your brand, the next step is to identify the potential of the market you will be serving. This is where you can talk about competitors, how there is a need for your brand, and the buying power your audience has that investors will miss out on if they don't come on board.

Finally, your implementation and financials should be very detailed since they will explain precisely what steps you will take with your newfound investment. Ideally map out what things will be put in place at least in the next three years to show that you're thinking ahead. This should outline the resources and operational procedures you'll need to bring pieces to life, including hiring interns and staff, renting a space, buying production materials, and marketing. This is all crucial to identifying how much it will cost to start and also what you will need to grow.

Then you can get into the financials, with an income statement listing your start-up expenditure and cash-flow statements month after month to show what funding you will need to keep the lights on. Too often, designers estimate that they need a certain amount, only to realize that they have orders to fill but no money to buy the materials to produce and deliver them. You'll also use this section to project how your business will grow through sales, against the costs of delivering that growth. Don't underestimate hiring a financial adviser even if just to help put your plan together. It can be a vital reality check of what your up-front costs are and how much revenue you're expecting. Financial advisers can give you guidance on what's possible now versus what's worth waiting for.

An example of a start-up expenditure would look something like this:

From the below analysis, I need an estimate of $240,000 to start and run my collection. It should be noted that the bulk of capital would be used to pay employees' salaries for a period of six months, lease a facility for an entire year, and acquire the textiles needed to make the highest-quality collection.

The key areas where we intend to spend our start-up capital are:

- Inventory of textiles, materials, office supplies, and design accessories: $100,000
- Leasing a facility for the period of one year: $25,000
- Website and social media creation: $2,500
- Operational cost for the first six months of salaries: $75,000
- Obtaining licenses and permits as well as accounting software: $1,250
- Cost of hiring a business consultant: $1,500
- Marketing promotion expenses: $7,437
- Insurance coverage for workers' compensation: $7,437
- Other start-up expenses (computers, printers, phones): $2,000

- Grand opening party: $3,000
- Miscellaneous: $14,875

This breakdown should help investors feel more comfortable with how much and why they're giving you money and see the longevity potential of what you're trying to create. It's also worth noting that the fashion industry has changed so much that "success" is not just one thing anymore—of course it means to be critically acclaimed and for people to respect your creativity, but it also entails having a brand that the public is interested in and that commercially sees sales and profits. Use your business plan as a way to decide how you see your brand and how it will be sustainable over time.

Once you've completed your business plan, think of this as the foundation on which you will build your business. It reveals how you will finance your business, what kind of investment you need, and how to allocate capital once you get it. Essentially each season, or when you come out with a collection, your sales should increase as your brand profile grows, but your up-front costs to create will be higher since you'll likely have more team members, want to use better fabrics, etc. The money you've earned from any previous sales won't sustain you to continue to create and hopefully grow, so you'll need multiple streams of financing.

Most people who have grown up in the fashion world have come from a privileged background and have access to hundreds of thousands of dollars from a family member or friend, which is why it's so common for designers to come from connected families. It is much easier to obtain money if your social circle is comprised of millionaires than if you're a struggling, broke college student living with five roommates. These are the realities. No, it's not fair.

If you're starting out as a designer with no contacts, there are a lot of different fashion funds, sponsorships, and collaborations, like the CFDA/Vogue Fashion Fund, Woolmark Prize, and more, but you can also try to get a bank loan or investors who want to own a percentage of your business for a larger payout. Investors range from angel, venture capital, and equity investors. The breakdown differentiates because angel and venture capital investors are simply people who recognize your potential but expect returns, usually in five to seven years. Private investors who have a high net worth and expertise in business are usually people who have become close friends with a brand and have a personal interest in seeing it succeed.

Either way, you should look for an investor who really believes in the ethos of the brand and is willing to give you time to grow. This person could potentially become part owner, be part of core decisions that you're making, and ask to be updated on how their investment is growing, so it should be someone you trust. If you cannot find an investor, a loan from a family friend or bank would allow you to maintain control of everything without giving away ownership of the brand. But it can be hard to find a family friend with a spare hundred thousand dollars or more. And it's not easy to meet the requirements for a loan at a bank since fashion design is a very risky business. You'll also have to pay the money back with interest in one to five years, depending on your credit score. Payments have to be paid every month.

Securing financing and taking time to think strategically about how money will be distributed is similar to putting down flooring—if you don't do it just right, everything that comes later will fall through. It may take time to get the money you need to get things going, and usually you won't get a big lump sum up front even if it's from an investor. So if you get only $10,000 in the first round, you have to think strategically how to use that amount and to make it last as long as you can. Even if you receive the amount that you initially requested, something will inevitably go wrong. Be financially prepared for that to happen a million times. It can feel a bit like the game Whac-A-Mole, tackling one thing with another crisis popping up the next second, but that's why having the firm foundation and knowing what's most important will help with decision-making. At this stage, it's essentially all about sacrifices to make production and sales flow.

CREATIVES OFTEN SKIP FIGURING out how their pieces will be manufactured. They assume if the ideas are there and a sample or two is made, then everything will fall into place. They will magically find someone to bring the entire collection to life for customers. The exact opposite is true. Will you manufacture by hand, in a factory, in large or small quantities, locally or internationally? If you built a firm foundation and installed the most beautiful marble-tile flooring and walls made of gold, it would mean nothing if the roof wasn't properly shingled because everything inside would get ruined regardless how beautiful it is.

Learn the lesson early—you can have a tight business plan, and even secure funding, but if pieces are not produced with quality and delivered to the consumer in a timely and economic manner, it is all for nothing. The choice of fabrics you can source and afford, and the complexities of patterns, will depend on the strength of your team and what makes the most logistical sense. Ideally your production will flow smoothly, but always leave room for error. Once the pattern is sent to your production team, they will create samples. The fabric in the samples could pull a certain way you don't like, or maybe it's not as dramatic as you imagined it would be, which means there will be more alterations and thus more time and money spent. Always give yourself more time and money than you think is necessary.

Most industry veterans recommend using your network, asking retailers, buyers, and people who understand textiles, about a cost-effective manufacturer from the beginning. Manufacturing can be very challenging and delay your entire process. Preferably, you want a manufacturer that's local so you can oversee on-site. Of course, using a local producer always costs more. After design prototypes for each piece are made to show construction guidelines, you should still be doing your own quality-control check to make sure pieces are made up to par. If you are producing a small amount, be prepared for higher fees—an average of a 50 percent margin at whole-sale and 70 percent in retail—and to make an up-front deposit to secure production even though you won't be receiving money from e-commerce orders or retailers for a while.

Stay nimble and flexible. You may want to make a dress in crepe chiffon that is elegant and slightly sheer, but if the price of the material in the color you want goes up or the factory you've decided to use doesn't have that particular fabric you may have to adjust and use a dif-ferent fabric or color to keep costs down. It's an endless dance, but stick to your animating vision.

It may seem as if there's no point in being a designer if you're not able to make the most amazing pieces in the best fabrics, but if you're making a large collection using incredibly expensive fabrics, you'll see your money run out faster than you can say *bankruptcy*. It can be tedious and frustrating to make creative sacrifices, but planning what fabrics you'll use at certain price points for each section of your collection will ultimately save you time and money.

At the same time, you should be thinking about sales and ways to increase revenue. I think of this step as installing the plumbing, electrical wiring, and drywall in a house. This will allow your house to function day in and day out, guaranteeing that you not only have something beautiful but also something making your business functional.

In today's economy you really have to build up a strong presence with social media, a consumer base, and a fair amount of red-carpet runs with celebrities for e-commerce and brick-and-mortar stores to reach out about buying your pieces wholesale. It's much more of a gamble now than it used to be, especially for emerging designers, because how people shop now has changed so drastically. From being open to spending thousands of dollars on a cool, new designer people now want to feel like those thousands of dollars are well spent on a brand that has longevity in both name and style. Which is why, more than ever, designers are leaning toward direct-to-consumer (D2C) marketing. Under this model, a strong brand can grow in popularity and keep costs down by eliminating the middleman, allowing for bigger profit margins. Look at D2C disruptors like Everlane and Warby Parker.

Some veterans in the industry still respect a traditional fashion show with big-name models. But with the accessibility of social media, it's no longer a requirement. There are tons of other effective ways to present your collection to customers and the press. It may seem as though a show doesn't cost much to produce if you do it on a smaller scale, but remember it's not just about producing the clothing—it's also the production of the event, hair and makeup artists, models, and styling fees. Increasingly, alternatives are "presentations" that last a couple of hours in a gallery space, capsule collections with other brands or e-commerce retailers to get more hype, pop-up shops at a temporary retail space, and trunk shows that allow designers to bring their collection to a boutique or retailer for a special in-shop showing that lasts up to eight weeks. All these options are more affordable and give you the opportunity to have one-on-one face time with the ever-important buyers and consumers.

Just as it's in your best interest to get a financial adviser to assess your spending, it's also wise to get a second opinion about the styling of your collection. Whether you do a presentation or social media campaign, it matters how the pieces are put together. Styling takes your pieces and turns them into stories. It demonstrates how things are actually worn, creating looks that elevate your brand. The concept of styling your own collection may seem like an easy thing to do, but it pays to have a third

party, someone with a fresh pair of eyes, combine different pieces together, bring out certain colors and textures,
and give the collection a new light. A good stylist can
reveal something about your work you hadn't previously
seen, adding a new dimension to your work.

It's also worth considering how fragile the relation-
ship between editors and designers is and what that
means for your business. Most designers and editors get
to know one another from being in the same spaces and
appreciating the other's work or following each other on
social media. But just because an editor likes your work
as a designer, it doesn't mean they are going to shoot
your product or give you a full-page profile. Politics are
always at play, and advertisers who pay to be featured in
publications get priority. Too often as a market editor, I
saw new labels spending all their money to advertise with
magazines, or having an elaborate show and not realizing that there was little return on investment for them
at that point. Just because a runway show is full doesn't
mean the right people are there to make connections
with your brand, give you publicity, and more customers. And the same is true for advertising—if editors
aren't genuinely interested in the products sold by the
advertiser, they're going to get placement but probably

not one they're too excited about. Especially with print sales for magazines down, there's always the possibility of a retailer sponsoring a cover or a brand contractually securing its full look on the cover of a publication. In my experience, it's always a balancing act of keeping advertisers happy but also sprinkling in new talent or designers editors genuinely love.

Assuming you don't have millions of dollars to spend on advertising in the beginning stages, the best use of any money and time you have for PR and marketing is to focus on creating a strong brand DNA with a distinct personality on social media and making your own direct-to-consumer pipeline through e-commerce or social media. I've always been a firm believer that your social media presence should feel authentic and make people want to be interested in not only the pieces you're selling but also the lifestyle of every part of your brand. Even if it's just sandals, it can't be solely about the sandals—your sandals have to make people feel as if they are being transported to somewhere, exotic or luxurious, in their imagination that fits in your brand's storytelling. The cadence in which you post, the quality of your images, and the tone in your captions are completely up to you. Create a narrative around your brand through your content. My only recommendation is consistency. You don't have to post every single day, but your brand name should be popping up on consumers' feeds every couple of days if you want to keep their attention. Your engagement with followers is arguably more important than an ad or magazine placement because you are able to instantly communicate with people on how much a new item is or if you're announcing a new product. Since editors and stylists are always on the hunt for a trendy, untapped creative, big name, having a tight edit on who you present yourself as on social media will increase the amount of people in the industry who reach out to you, eager to know more. Your social media platforms can help grow sales and awareness with a velocity unheard of even ten years ago. It is a crucial, indispensable piece of your marketing. Don't underestimate its power, but also don't let it be an all-consuming pursuit.

It takes most designers years to be able to get retail buyers' attention. Even if you are just selling pieces on your own e-commerce site, it's imperative to watch the data. Track unit sales, margins, and returns. The data is a direct reflection of what your customers are interested in and how much you're making. If you work backward from the retail price and include things like shipping fees, sample costs, and development costs, then you're a lot less likely to lose money.

As you'll read in the next few chapters, every designer is unique and builds their respective brand differently. Again, there's no uniform template. But the common thread for all three designers I mentioned in the introduction is the core pieces that they are known for that are reinvented in new ways but still allow for a solid foundation. It can be a general aesthetic, a signature item, or something that's priced moderately depending on your preference; the only factor that matters is that it be original so people feel as if they can get that look, that piece, that vibe from only you. For Rogers it's his ruffled, dramatic evening wear; for McCharen-Tran it's bold, inclusive swimwear; and for Assoulin it's elegant, voluminous tops. These are all items that, truthfully, the designers may be tired of re-creating, but they're part of each brand's ethos—accessible pieces that people who don't even understand fashion are interested in buying. From there, it's usually a mix of wardrobe staples reinvented, like a dress that always sells out or a great pair of tailored pants in new fabrics and colors. This is a way for you to make things you know people are interested in and price them more expensively, so even if people have purchased an earlier version, they're likely to buy it again if they love wearing it. And last, interspersed are seasonal items that bring in new elements to the collection that can be a mix of things that are purely editorial or that you're hoping a celebrity wears on a red carpet. Too much clutter and noise can drown out the beauty in pieces, making it harder for everyone to digest what you're trying to say about yourself.

Just like a house, your brand will still need upkeep once it's built; there is never a moment of being done since there is always a new collection, a new round of funding, or a new vision to evolve the brand. There will never be a day when there isn't something to fix or update. But if you don't take the time to make sure your brand is built on a firm foundation, like many brands before, it will crumble.

Hopefully all this has helped give some background information on all the little things you should bear in mind before embarking on a journey as a designer. These fundamentals allow you to realize what makes the most sense for where you are and where you'd like to go. It's imperative to seek perspective and advice from people who have lived through this process. On paper it can seem simple and straightforward. The actual day in and day out is another story.

In the following chapters, you'll read the intimate stories of emerging as a designer from Christopher John Rogers, the lessons on building your brand from Becca McCharen-Tran of Chromat, and the keys to growing your ideas into a formidable business from Rosie Assoulin.

2

HOW TO EMERGE

One could argue that becoming a fashion designer is never easy. We've gone through the early-stage logistics of things you'll need to keep in mind before launching. And we've established that while planning and foresight go an incredibly long way, everyone's early career takes shape differently. This chapter shows how Christopher John Rogers has emerged from an unknown designer with a love of anime and Pokemon, to dressing celebrities like Michelle Obama, Cardi B, and Tessa Thompson. His story will not only help answer questions about the challenges of being a new designer but also help you make decisions with confidence. There is no right or wrong way to get your brand out there. It's a balancing act of experimenting, reconfiguring, and refining. The process of creating your brand can be maddening and frustrating, but there is so much joy to it. There's no one better to learn from than the incredible Rogers.

I don't remember the exact moment when I found out who Rogers was, but I do remember the feeling of excitement when I saw his dramatic and feminine creations all over social media. The easiest way I can describe it is that his was the most poetic iteration of clothing I'd ever seen—it had emotion and its own feelings. I had to know more. The voluminous dresses, references to cultural moments, and commitment to bold colors were so intriguing. Newer designers tend to try and recreate things they love from iconic brands like Dior or Balenciaga, but, Rogers's vision—his shapes, color palettes, and silhouettes—are completely his own. Rogers

became interested in fashion at a young age, drawn to anything graphic from Digimon to Power Rangers. Born and raised in Baton Rouge, Louisiana, Rogers started by drawing his own characters. "I remember in elementary school, I was drawing comics with one of my friends [who] asked why the character always wore the same thing. And I got curious and started to investigate different clothing I could draw, and how clothing could change not only the way someone looks but the way someone feels about themselves." In fifth grade he discovered one of my former employers, Style.com (which has now merged into Vogue Runway), where all exclusive collections and interviews with their designers premiere. By high school, Rogers had learned how to sew, begging his parents for a sewing machine to make a collection for his high school fashion show. He ended up hand-sewing everything since he couldn't figure out how to work the machine his parents got him. As luck would have it, one of the parents of a fellow student came up to him after the show, complimented him on his work, and offered to show him how to sew more professionally.

After graduating from high school in 2012, Rogers attended Savannah College of Art and Design (SCAD), and, as he puts it "went into school kind of cocky." Since

Rogers already knew how to sew, he took inspiration from his Baptist upbringing—specifically from churchgoers who wore feathered hats and monochromatic suits—and also felt more self-assured in his perspective than others who seemed to be newly figuring out fashion. He vividly remembers one of his professors telling him, "This is shit . . . your clothing is not nearly as good as you think it is." But it was the tough love that he needed. "It was hard for me to get acclimated to the fact that I don't know everything, and it was really a humbling experience for me. It's a lesson that I still try and take with me."

Most of his classes were three hours long, with only a few absences a semester allowed before a mandatory failing grade. "It was more about ideas and pushing myself forward because I knew the collection I dreamed of making; it was more so what it took to get there. It was a lot of time spent on construction, sketching, and conceptualizing." After internships at Chris Benz, Tanya Taylor, and Rosie Assoulin, Rogers felt ready to present his ideas in full. "My senior collection I focused on being the designer that consistently, no matter what the season is, no matter what the trends are, would do my own thing, and make things that I'm obsessed with, so I made thirty garments in six weeks."

Rogers describes his senior collection as "a mix of indigenous tribes, mid-century couture, and traditional tailoring" He felt as if his references and obsessions were something his professors didn't understand since they were so specific. Rogers persisted with his obsessions, and they have proven to be things others are obsessed with too. "I always come back to [loving color] and taking up space . . . whether it be through volume or the emotion and femininity. I don't think there needs to be some kind of dichotomy in order for it to be relevant," he says.

Though he was personally happy with the senior collection show, no press showed up, and no stores emailed him to get his pieces in, as he thought would happen. There were great resources at SCAD, and many alumni in fashion, but he was interested in working for smaller, more creative designers only. He knew the kind of collection he wanted to make. He wanted to learn about starting his own business instead of working for a large company like Ralph Lauren or Michael Kors. "The places I wanted to work at . . . it's not easy to continually hire new talent. That's the struggle of design school—every year the pool of talent gets bigger, and you're released into the wild with so few jobs available." Therefore, as soon as he graduated, Rogers went home for two months to save money and moved to New York in the summer of 2016. To pay his bills, he got a job waiting tables at a restaurant while frantically emailing stylists in the hope that they needed an assistant or that they wanted to use his clothing to shoot for an editorial. "Things slowly started to happen," he remembers. "I had one sample set, so not much to go around to stylists, but people were pulling things for shoots and returning them late or ripped—which is part of it—but I wasn't ready for the hassle of it all."

He still wasn't hearing back from applications—and had put out a wide net, from applying to entry-level jobs in production to patternmaking and merchandising. "I wasn't getting responses and I thought I did a good job in school. My portfolio was solid, but I knew it was because my vision was so specific and people tend to look for someone more amenable." A lot of the feedback he would get was that there wasn't enough black or contemporary pieces, and potential employers would ask, "Why are you even applying for a job here if you have your own vision?" Rogers would answer, "Because I need the money." Looking back on this time, Rogers never really wanted to work for someone else, but unless you come from a family with a trust fund or have investors straight out of college, you need a healthy bank account to create.

Finally, one of his applications recieved a reply—a position at Diane von Furstenberg (DVF), working with Jonathan Saunders, as an associate knitwear designer. "I had no prior experience in knitwear," he says, laughing. "But I was very up front that this is my portfolio, I have no experience in this particular aspect, but I'm a hard worker." Saunders took a chance on him, and now Rogers is able to do knits for himself, a skill he wouldn't have thought to acquire had the opportunity not come his way.

"Looking back on that time in my career, I didn't understand the depths of how the industry works, or how much nepotism is involved," he says. "When you leave school and get a job as a junior person, you're just doing somebody else's work and bringing their vision to life. And that's everybody, no matter what field, but in fashion design I think you really learn about the operations of how things work, and mistakes I didn't want to make with my own brand."

His day-to-day responsibilities at DVF included making copies, arranging styling and mood boards, sketching, and sewing. Since his own experience had been doing the draping and sewing all on his own, it was definitely a learning curve to work at a company that outsourced production and required Rogers to be much more technical on the design end. "I had to technically write down all the specs of each garment, and everything had to be exactly right since you were giving the information to people overseas to create batches of clothing. It was a lot!" Ultimately Rogers got to sit in on design fittings with Saunders and the DVF team, and put pieces together for pre-styling to see how they would look on the runway. He was now working with the team in an intimate manner. "I really got to see so much firsthand because there were only a handful of designers besides Johnathan, so we were making a large amount of things in a very small space. They were elevated but still commercial, which I liked because it meant that a lot of different people could wear the clothing instead of just models."

While he was working at DVF, his own debut collection for Spring 2019 made more waves than he thought it would. He would sketch and hand-sew creations from fabric he bought in the Garment District on sale, working at night in the apartment he shares with two roommates, and thought of it as an opportunity to pour out creatively all that he had been holding in that wasn't on-brand or a fit at DVF. Because he spent time with so many people in the industry at work, he was able to make connections to fashion editors at events or during press appointments at DVF, so when the time came for his own line, he was able to tap into his own network. He called his collection "A Southern Sunday Best," which featured clashing plaid prints, monochromatic looks, church hats that could win awards, and voluminous evening wear. It combined his love of bold colors with subdued patterns, putting his own spin on tame pieces and making them more whimsical. The collection got picked up on Vogue.com, *WWD*, *Elle*, and more publications because it was practically everywhere on social media the day it debuted, and people couldn't believe he was so young and largely unknown. Because of his designs' popularity, it ultimately led to Rogers's leaving DVF to focus full-time on his own brand.

Because Rogers needed money, he started doing a lot more custom pieces, taking on the kind of commission work he wasn't able to do when he was working at DVF. He also supplemented his income with odd jobs like tailoring on set for photo shoots. Rogers is now preparing for a show that features only his designs in September 2019. He admits even though this is what he has always dreamed of and wanted, it's been tough. "The money is always the biggest struggle, but also just knowing what to do with the structure and actual business side is hard to figure out." For now the plan is to continue to do custom work to be able to fund the collections, get the business plan out to investors, and apply to funds like the CFDA/Vogue Fashion Fund in order to get more capital and connections. "Right now I have a goal of money that I think I would need to create, but I also have a number in mind if those things fall through. On average, the last collection I made cost $7,000, so no matter what, if I have two dollars or two thousand dollars, the collection's going to be amazing."

So far he has been sticking to presentations instead of shows. He aims to do what's best for that collection. "It's about doing what feels right," he says. "One thing that I'm learning is that there shouldn't be or that there isn't any pressure to do anything just because people expect it from me. One season if we just want to shoot a look book, great. One season if we want to put the money and production into doing a runway show, great. Whatever feels right for us at the time is what we'll do."

Even though he's had to be scrappy, Rogers credits his relentless approach to his brand to seeing firsthand how designers spend hundreds of thousands of dollars on fabric and waste money. "I don't need a ton of money to make everything. And people get hung up on buying a ton of fabric from Italy so that you can say it's from Italy that you may or may not use but you can usually find the same thing in New York. And on top of the fact that I make everything here, I can make a quality sample for less than a thousand dollars."

His daily schedule is a bit different, dividing his time between working on custom orders and constructing new pieces. "Since I make everything, it takes a long time to actually create all the clothing. It's different every day which is a bit scary for me since I got so used to the consistency of a nine-to-five job." When I ask if he feels more pressure because he's on his own now, he quickly says, "No the pressure I feel is from myself and the things I want to do." In reality, the well-received pieces he has become known for were made while he was working full-time. So the hope is that given that he now has the time and space to create freely, his work will be even better.

It's a rarity for a young designer to emerge as young and as fast as Rogers did. At twenty-five, he is still relatively fresh out of college—yet his name is already buzzing in the industry. His clothing is so beautiful and captivating in nature, and it didn't take long for stylists to DM him on Instagram and ask him to loan pieces for celebrity clients. Celebrities like Cardi B wore his pieces to award shows, SZA in a music video with Kendrick Lamar, and Tracee Ellis Ross, Tessa Thompson, and Michelle Obama to various red-carpet events. Rogers's popularity proves the point that having something to say is always the foundation, no matter if you use church hats or haute couture to say it. The sudden success of his custom pieces and dramatic evening wear has laid the path for Rogers to have cash flow and continue to be a surprise hit as a designer.

But with the shine came the pressures of being a Black designer in an industry that mostly cares about inclusivity on a surface level. I am cautious about people in fashion truly caring about diverse voices. Big fashion houses tend to do only what's necessary to stay relevant and profitable. There is little room for integrity because capital is key. When I broach the issue with Rogers, he says, "My favorite things is when I meet people and they pull my work or have seen my work on social media and say, 'Oh, I didn't even know that you were black!'" For Rogers, his experience as a black man has been unique and special, just like everyone else on the planet. His references of growing up in church, of Southern decadence and polish are his own, but he doesn't feel the pressure to perform it. "I like the fact that maybe people are uncomfortable when they meet me. I'm happy with the work that I'm doing because it's rooted so much in blackness but it's not directly about being black. It's about me being a black person and I happen to make these clothes."

Though he has a million things on his mind, there's something freeing in hearing Rogers be so steadfast in his views. And even though he may not see it as an act of defiance, the way he embraces all the specific nuances of the things he likes—the way he leans into his own voice and tunes out others—is what young designers need to do to survive. He's been able to talk to designers like Kerby Jean-Raymond of Pyer Moss who won the CFDA/Vogue Fashion Fund in 2018, whom Rogers calls "a great champion, and super supportive" and is using the small network he has to move forward.

In brainstorming his September 2019 collection, Rogers must balance what he knows his customers want while surprising them. He recognized that people were responsive to strawberry-red and pinks, so in this upcoming collection he'll be exploring ideas of circular, spherical shapes in new ways. "People have loved the ruffles that I do and I'm done with it, but I'm trying to find a way to reinterpret it, and make it feel fresh but not reduce the drama, so maybe deflating the ruffle on one side or playing with a multicolor situation will make sense." Like most contemporary designers in the market, his pieces range in price from $350 for a blouse to $1,390 for an evening dress. Some of his pieces are sold on Forty Five Ten, but mostly everything is direct-to-consumer from his website. People may assume that because he is an emerging designer his prices should be lower, but knowing your worth and infrastructure is important. Rogers is selling things that are made in his own house, so they're naturally going to be much more expensive because there is no way to automate production. He is literally hand-sewing garments one by one. The time, labor, and production costs all skyrocket. Rogers puts it best by saying, "You always need more than you think you do. But at the same time, you can do less with what you have."

The next stage of building his brand, in addition to generating more revenue and throwing it back into the company, was being able to hire people other than his roommates. He admits that first seeing designers with more access and funding felt unfair. He now focuses on the future. "For the longest time I've complained about how things weren't fair but the fact that I know all these things about the construction of clothing, that allows me to achieve things no one else can," he says. "I'm very into a gradual climb and I'm okay with things taking time. We've gotten requests from places like *Vogue*, and nothing's happened yet but even the request says I'm on my way."

There are so many points in Rogers's story where most people would have given up—he didn't have the pedigree and fancy background of having connections in the industry, or the money to endlessly fun his dreams, but he did have his talent and relentless approach to making his brand successful. He is a designer who has emerged in his own way instead of trying to please people and hoping that they like his work, which has allowed him to claim his own space in the fashion industry. Rogers has taught me invaluable lessons that led me to further explore what it takes to build your brand over the span of a decade, like Becca McCharen-Tran of Chromat.

3

HOW TO BUILD

After learning more about Rogers finding his way, it only made sense to follow the journey of Becca McCharen-Tran. The in-between years of building a sustainable business that conforms to your standards and continues to thrive is rarely written about. That's because it's a grinding, often unglamorous process filled with setbacks and growing pains. McCharen-Tran has already emerged as an established designer; her brand Chromat is taken seriously as an authority in the industry. In the span of a decade she's been nominated for a CFDA Swarovsky Award, sold collections at various retailers, and regularly has shows during New York Fashion Week. This chapter will explore what she's done in order to keep her business running while also securing a strong presence on and off the runway.

A decade may not seem like a long time, but in fashion speak that's more than enough time to see a lot of trends and businesses pass away. That's why Chromat is still worth celebrating. Ten years in, it is still one of the most coveted shows to attend during New York Fashion Week. Somehow, in every collection, the luxury swimsuit and bodywear brand intersects the worlds of fashion and inclusivity with an energy and eye like no one else. McCharen-Tran's collections mainly feature swimsuits, separates, body-encapsulating cages, sportswear, and lingerie; all styles are innovative and created with cutting-edge technical fabrics. Her designs embrace not only a variety of sizes but also of genders, sexualities, disabilities, ethnicities, and everything in between. McCharen-Tran has oriented her brand around human emotion and marginalized cultures. This has allowed her to tap into the emotional connection innate in the shopping experience.

Brick-and-mortar stores aren't nearly as popular as they used to be—in fact, shops are closing at record-high numbers. But think about how many times you've tried something on, only for it to look terrible in the dressing-room lighting and not fit properly. Experiences like that stay with people for a lifetime. If you can change the experience then you can change the emotional response that goes along with shopping for something as personal as a bathing suit. That's become Chromat's magnum opus. Most people wouldn't readily think to buy a swimsuit online in fear that it wouldn't fit properly, but because consumers know they can go to Chromat, a brand that's formed a community around feeling good no matter what size you are, they don't even think twice about buying.

Being in the Chromat studio nearly brings me to tears. The mannequins are size inclusive, the photos and messages about the brand's DNA on the walls are about empowerment and sexiness instead of clichéd storytelling, and there are powerful signs of protest everywhere. One in particular catches my eye. It's titled POOL RULES in a nod to Chromat's swimsuit campaign for last year, and lists things like INTOLERANCE NOT TOLERATED,

FOOD-SHAMING NOT PERMITTED, and SCARS + STRETCH MARKS WELCOME, all heavy-hitting topics most fashion brands would never dream of talking about let alone putting on a sign. It's this kind of branding that comes natural to McCharen-Tran and is part of who she is as an individual. But her beliefs and values say something that expands far past the runway, enabling her to connect with so many people across the world.

"The way people feel neglected," McCharen-Tran says as she shakes her head, "because they haven't had everything that straight-sized people have . . . or that there's been so few resources—it is a lifetime of neglect and second-best options." And acknowledging that "neglect" allowed Chromat to become what it is today—it doesn't follow trends, fads, or hype. McCharen-Tran's made it the norm to be inclusive in everything she does. And nothing is put-on or inauthentic. It comes from an unwavering sincerity and commitment to values.

Raised in Lynchburg, Virginia, the dream started for McCharen-Tran when she was studying architecture. "I loved architectural design," she admits, "but fashion for me was really a fun way to build something on a smaller scale. You can design a dress in two hours, versus building it can take you years or decades to really see your vision come to life." You can see the influence of architecture in the way every piece of hers is made—a swimsuit so precise in its cutouts and fit or a corset that seems as if it were deconstructed and put together again in the most modern manner. The speed and immediacy of seeing her creations attracted McCharen-Tran to the fashion world, but she chalks up her career to a little experiment. On the side, after work, she started to do little fashion shows in Virginia. She met a coworker who had a family member employed in fashion in New York and had connections to pop-up stores.

McCharen-Tran spent her nights going home and sewing cage corsets and bustiers made with materials from her local Joann Fabrics and Crafts store, shipping them to New York pop-up shops in the hope that someone would see a spark of talent. Eventually she quit her job assisting at an architecture firm and moved to New York. To her surprise, she started getting a lot of orders since the pop-ups she worked with turned into brick-and-mortar retail stores that started doing wholesale.

She's earned acclaim, recognition, and awards. She's been able to break boundaries by dressing some of the biggest celebrity names like Beyoncé, Madonna, and Nicki Minaj. She was named by *Forbes* as one of the "People Who Are Reinventing the World" in its 2014 "30 Under

30" list. Since Chromat's inception in 2010, the business has gone through drastic changes internally, morphing into different versions to survive. After all, it can be an impossible task to bridge the worlds of fashion and technology with substance, consider best practices for the environment, and sustain sales in an oversaturated market like swimwear. But somehow McCharen-Tran has found a way to stay responsive to societal changes and stay innovative with body-enhancing creations.

"When I first began, I was super experimental, just thinking about architecture and material research, and not thinking about wearable garments as much," she says. "It was more just like how can we design for the body in cool new ways." But in time she also had to learn the balance between being a creative with a desirable brand and what makes sense for the overall health of the brand.

This is the key difference in emerging and building—maturity not only in how you spend money but also in realizing how the choices you make every single day will affect your business, potentially for years to come. McCharen-Tran could have easily continued with most of her experiments and let her ego take over, but instead she looked at the brand pragmatically to find that middle ground between her dreams and what consumers want.

"You have to sell clothes and figure out what people really want to wear," she admits, even though I know this is a struggle for designers to contend with. The conflict over being a creative and being financially successful as a designer has been around since the beginning of global apparel companies like LVMH and PVH. The intersection of art and commerce creates a tension that's come up with Raf Simons's departure after less than two years at Calvin Klein, Alexander Wang's collaboration with Balenciaga that ended in less than three years, and, conversely perhaps the most financially successful, Alessandro Michele's transformation of Gucci that's paved the way for unique creative direction and exponential growth as a brand.

Like most designers, McCharen-Tran hit bumps in the road—like finances and figuring out which core pieces she should continue to create to keep consumers interested—in order to refine the Chromat brand. McCharen-Tran insists she's figured most of it out the hard way. "We were doing, like, all sorts of cages, and then we started filling in more of the little bits around the cage, so we did lingerie, sportswear, swim, and shoes," she lists. And after Chromat started to expand into different product categories, it came to the point where it was doing too much— a step that is part of the growing and building process.

There was a desire to expand the business exponentially, but what works for other brands is no guarantee that it'll work for yours. "We ended up just really changing course and focusing on swim, because that was the product that was the most commercial success." McCharen-Tran isn't the first person to make swimwear, and there have been other designers with similar ideas, but none have executed them as well as Chromat. Every single show is filled with so much positivity and excitement. People want to see different kinds of bodies in intricate pieces. Her ability to take a small amount of fabric and turn it into a movement intersecting body positivity and fashion is unmatched.

Swimwear was an organic path for the brand, and, as she says, "a good piece of the puzzle." It allowed Chromat to design quality bodywear in an intriguing manner while staying true to the brand's values and mission statement—*feel good in your own skin*. At its core, Chromat has always cared about representation, which differentiated it from other brands. Eventually, the models and customers who were dedicated to the brand became a unique selling point in an oversaturated market.

McCharen-Tran quickly noticed that her shows were starkly different from others during New York Fashion Week. It was what she was expressing with her line that caught people's attention. "I would be really into the idea of what the collection meant and what the colors and inspiration meant, and all the reviews would say, 'A plus-sized model walked the runway.'" With no mention of the clothes or the thought behind each piece's creative process, it was shock to both the industry and to her. But what Chromat set the stage for was the idea of transcending clothing for just the sake of clothing—fashion with a conscience and substance.

As she reflects on the past ten years, she says, "I think I'm lucky in a sense that what we do reflects our real lives. The reason that we had all these models, who are all different from all different places, because that was our friend group of the artists and the people that we worked alongside." She's made efforts to surround herself with a diverse community, to which she credits her brand's growth. "It all reflects your real life—if you're a white designer who only hangs out with white people, then you probably won't even know a black person to ask to be a model in your look book. You won't even have someone who is in a wheelchair in your friend group or social circle. It all shows on the runway, and it shows who you're centering in your own life."

When McCharen-Tran was a finalist in the CFDA/Vogue Fashion Fund, she was able to connect with people in the industry to garner practical advice on how to expand her brand. One conversation in particular still makes her laugh. "I asked a designer when he was going to have plus-sized models in his runway show, and he scoffed that he didn't want to seem like he was jumping on a trend instead of it being something inherent to his brand values!" But she did walk away from the event having met with Lynn Yaeger, contributing fashion editor to Vogue.com and former fashion reporter at the *Village Voice* for thirty years, who was an instant and early champion of Chromat.

While the financial situation for most designers isn't transparent, McCharen-Tran set out to get to the bottom of things so that she wouldn't fall into the trap of blowing through all her money. "I sat down with Lynn and just told her, 'I don't get it, all these designers I look up to. You read their biography, and they have a $50,000 donation from their parents just for the first month,'" she admits. "The bottom line in the beginning was that if a season didn't sell that was a wrap, and over the years I've made that mistake and had to let people go and it was back to me working out of my bedroom because I love this work." Over time one of the key lessons for McCharen-Tran was honing in on what to present each season so that she could see a return in order to keep creating. At the same time, she needed capital coming in so that she wasn't so dependent on a collection selling so poorly that it would cause her to go out of business. The truth is that brands need to stay relevant even when there isn't much hype or something to dazzle your consumers. The longevity and loyalty of your customers is what matters. You could be the new "it" designer your first couple of seasons, and then fade into someone people used to talk about *very* quickly. It's a tightrope, but if you want to last you have to create a brand that people come back to over and over again, with or without something new to entice them. That comes from having something to say.

I also think it greatly helped McCharen-Tran when she started to dig deep to figure out her own white privilege, blindness, and tokenism she unknowingly took part in. The brand became more of a political lightning rod, creating a space where designers could have real dialogue about what's going on in the world instead of hiding behind the label. Chromat is a needed breath of fresh air in that way. Her most recent collection tackled the conversation of sustainability and how global warming and climate change need to be high on the agenda for designers since swimwear may one day become what we now know as ready-to-wear if Earth continues to get warmer and depleted of its natural resources. She also has had the debate of whether to keep plus-sized labeling, to which she now says, "I've been seeing a lot of conferences and panels about plus-sized things and models not wanting to be called plus-sized and just wanting to be models. But my opinion is that there should just be a way to categorize different-sized clothing for the ease of shopping, and erase the stigma and negative connotation of plus-sized instead."

Fat phobia is real, even if you're just walking outside your house on a Tuesday. But in the fashion industry it is rooted even deeper. The phobia becomes a feeling of hate. It derives from Eurocentric beauty ideals that have been handed down from generations of white CEOs to white fashion editors and white photographers. "There's just so much history, and the stigma is so real that there's so much to flip the script on," McCharen-Tran explains. But since she is so passionate about body positivity, it only makes sense that she is one of the people to spearhead its insertion in fashion. After all, according to CNN, the plus-sized retail market is worth more than $21 billion, so who better than Chromat to finally make it possible for people of all sizes to participate in fashion that feels luxurious?

In the early years, McCharen-Tran didn't see her own belief system as being an organic way to build Chromat. "We realized it was about changing the whole culture on how you feel about larger bodies. It's not just cutting some more sizes in your collection," she says. "Everyone needs to change, but it comes down to a matter of priorities." She repeats her point while showing me early designs.

She says that the worst thing a designer can do is make an ugly ill-fitting garment. When you see the lengths to which she goes to make sure all body types have equitable fabrication it's more than impressive, it's inspiring.

Even though Chromat has had models on the runway for five years, whenever the collection was brought to market, buyers were never interested in getting anything above a size large. McCharen-Tran participates in the traditional fashion calendar of showing every spring and summer. In this model buyers are purchasing one season in advance, looking for trends and standouts. Chromat was hardly ever considered. "In the past year we started going up to a 3X and 4X, but that was only possible because we had retail support from Nordstrom and 11 Honoré. They were the first retailers to ever buy 'curve' sizes from us."

The economics of being a designer is heightened for someone like McCharen-Tran because the more inclusive the brand, the more people assume that you should somehow be everything for everyone—not only inclusive but also accessible, affordable, and more. Now that she has swimwear available in sizing, customers seem to want it cheaper but still with great fabric and construction. That's nearly impossible. For instance, Chromat sells a printed zippered one-piece swimsuit in XS–3X at Nordstrom that looks a little sporty, a little bit Bond girl (i.e., has sex appeal), but it'll cost you $350, which is more than what most people are used to paying for swimwear. The customer has also gone through trauma since clothing ads, for generations, have been saying that plus-sized clothing should be transitional, instead of saying this is the size of your body and it deserves just as much love and attention as other body shapes. "We can't just do stuff because we want to—it's a matter of money," she says, "especially with a customer base that's been treated so poorly in the past, retail orders changed the game financially but at the same time we knew we had to make sure the fit was right."

"I was scared!" she goes on. "Our first collection I knew it wasn't going to be a one-hundred-percent perfect fit for everyone. But after we launched our first 'curve' sizes, we had a massive fit test with over a hundred people from sizes 0 to 30 to try on the whole collection." Just the thought of having a fit test for people to come in and try on clothes that have been on the runway leaves me baffled. Most designers care more about their vision and less about you fitting into the clothes. It's also a really efficient way of doing market research—seeing what people gravitate to and their reactions when they look in the mirror. Fit complaints and pricing queries can all be addressed for free out of love for the brand. Over the course of four days, McCharen-Tran and her team took data from each fitting. They shot a ton of pictures, took measurements, noted feedback on cup size, support, and fit. Most companies would pay millions of dollars to understand these nuances. "There's still a lot of ways that we do better for our plus-sized customers that we're continuing to add, but it's scary because it's not going to be perfect, especially because there is so much range in body shape."

Making inclusivity the status quo is undoubtedly what Chromat's legacy will be, but the clothes themselves are the crown jewels. "I would love someday for people to talk about the clothes," McCharen-Tran explains. "Lingerie is private, but swimwear is public, and it's public to consume. It's a real place of vulnerability that every person that wears swimwear goes through. And if there's anything that we can do to undo some of the societal pressure around bodies, then that's what we want to achieve."

If you learn anything from reading about Chromat, I hope the lesson is to find a way to do what you want to do regardless of the industry roadblocks. Take time to figure out how your personal ethos can be synonymous with the product and growth of the brand. When people think of Chromat, they think of clothing—but they support the brand not only because it's well made but also because they agree with the thinking behind Chromat. The brand boldly says to be kind to yourself, to your body, and to others—no matter who you are or your size. McCharen-Tran's identity is the kind of reality we all wish to live in. Her swimwear gives you that feeling every time you put it on.

4

HOW TO GROW

To get a well-rounded view of what it's like to be a fashion designer, this chapter follows the story of Rosie Assoulin. All things considered, Rogers and McCharen-Tran are still young designers. Assoulin has been in this industry for a long time—she's had more than a few false starts before truly committing. When she finally was ready to have something to say as a designer, she had ideas and strategies on how to build and evolve her brand into something distinct. She's had to learn how to emerge as a high-price ready-to-wear brand when she didn't have a name. She's had to learn how to grow that brand into a lifestyle that consumers would constantly crave. And even after successfully passing through these tiring stages, she's still evolving, expanding her playing field and reach as a brand. This chapter will delve into what it means to use all the tools in your belt and grow your business. It's one thing to emerge and get people to care about who you are and what you're selling. It's another to gain the lasting trust and loyalty of customers even when there's no hype. But if your brand isn't growing and you aren't thinking toward the future, something is dying, whether it be sales or general interest.

When I talk about growing your brand from a single collection to a reference point in culture, I don't want you to get the idea that the goal for every company is to be a global corporation with thousands of employees. The reality is that only historic fashion houses have that nowadays. And they are owned by even bigger multinational conglomerates. That is truly big business, a different universe that I won't be going into here.

Think less about the number of employees you have and more about the fact you will have to make risky adjustments that will shift the direction of your business. Because of the times we are in, if you stay doing the same thing, hoping things won't change, you're just not being realistic. The only way to grow is to be responsive, open to change, technologically oriented, and competitive. Assoulin has more than stepped up to the plate because she has consistently challenged herself to be innovative every season, and she hasn't once watered down her creativity. She's made it work.

When I was a fashion editor, it was no secret that other editors skipped a fair amount of shows during fashion week because their schedule was packed and, honestly, some were just a waste of time. But from the moment Assoulin started showing her work she has been one of the few must-see luxury designers. This past season at the September presentation, it was pouring torrential rain, and even though I was wearing a silk slip dress I still attended—soaked as much as a wet dog. Simply put, the way Assoulin makes everything easy to wear yet glamorous and elevated is hard to put into words. Everything feels special, fanciful, a bit romantic, but it also has this easy, wearable approach that makes you think, *I can pull that off.* Nothing is what it would be in the hands of other designers—instead of a printed maxi dress, Assoulin makes hers in vivid colors with voluminous sleeves so chic I almost forget how cheesy and music festival–esque most maxi dresses look.

While many new designers are considered emerging for longer than they'd prefer, Assoulin quickly jumped from being the new kid on the block to someone everyone in fashion wanted to know. But her journey to being coveted wasn't smooth. When she was young, Assoulin fell in love with fashion, playing in her mother's closet and drawing outfits. "When I was around thirteen or fourteen, my grandmother gave me her sewing machine that she used to make clothing for my mother and my aunt," she says. "My grandmother was the one who saw my passion for making clothes and that I had this healthy curiosity." From that point on, Assoulin spent hours in her room, cutting up old fabrics from the moment she got home from school to the moment she went to bed. She went to Yeshiva school, so everything from her collarbone to her ankles had to be covered. Assoulin turned this limitation into a challenge: to design something that was modest, scrappy, and creative.

"I got thrown out of Flatbush High School, probably

because I focused too much on staying up at night and sewing clothes," she admits. After that she did a host of internships, one with her mother-in-law, jewelry designer Roxanne Assoulin, whom she looked up to because she was the only woman she knew in the fashion industry with her own business. "Everybody has to find that person that you see yourself in or something you can relate to. And Roxanne was that for me. A lot of women I knew ran community organizations or stayed at home with their kids, but Roxanne was such a big mentor for me of someone working for themselves." Though Assoulin was probably too young to know at the time, mentorship like that she received can help greatly not just in having someone you know personally to talk to, but to help imagine a future and to get inspiration and ambition from. Her internship with this mentor clearly made all the difference in Rosie's determination to become a designer. I don't doubt it also contributed to the confidence it takes to go at it alone.

After a short stint studying at the Fashion Institute of Technology, Assoulin worked for Roxanne's jewelry line on the weekends at trade shows, hustling for work and trying to find her way. "At this point I had gotten fired a few times because all I wanted to do was do my own work making clothing, so Roxanne called me in her office and asked, 'What do you want to do with your life other than drive me crazy?' And I said, 'You know I really want to learn more about the clothing industry.'" As luck would have it, Assoulin wrote down the top ten designers she would love to work with, sent her résumé out to them, and got an internship at Oscar de la Renta. "I was so amazed by being there because it's still, to this day, incredibly rare to have a full working atelier in the French tradition (it's more common and affordable to outsource internationally), with everything from the draping, to the tailor, to the patternmakers and sample makers in New York City on Seventh Avenue."

Assoulin recollects many times throughout our conversation how unforgettable that experience was, and how it has shaped her thinking about how clothes are made and how the small details meaningfully affect your brand. After more than a year as an intern, nothing at the company opened up, so Assoulin went back to freelance designing, including working for a friend who was able to show Assoulin the behind-the-scenes aspect of running a small-scale fashion business.

"The next experience that changed my life was interning at Lanvin in Paris," she recalls. "It was just a time in my life that I can't unsee because of the techniques. And the quality of the fabrics and detailing were just out of this world. Everything that came out of that place you couldn't hold a candle to because it was that good," she remembers. "The beauty, the craft, the personal and authentic connection to every piece was so real." It's almost like seeing a dying art, but the experience at most European and French ateliers is much more precise and prestigious compared to what most American designers can provide because they depend more on outsourcing and cutting costs. There's a lot more history and care that's taken in creating clothing overseas, while most designers in America are producing clothing via a massive manufacturer.

But after the internship at Lanvin was over—because it was so magical and the reality of starting something on her own was fading—she buried the memories. "I got pregnant with my son, and I tried to start doing event planning and creating floral arrangements, and I had a good time doing it," she adds. "But I did this weird thing where I just tried to cut myself off from the fashion world because it was dark and depressing for me not to be able to release my creativity." At one point it got so bad that Assoulin didn't want to go outside because she was afraid she would get inspired and be frustrated not knowing what to do with her dreams. She found soalce by profusely sketching in notebooks and hiding them in her closet.

"About six or seven years ago, my parents started bugging me about it, and the people around me would just tell me to start and just do it and were supportive." During that time Assoulin was pregnant with her second child, so she spent her days working locally in the garment district, and at nights after she cooked dinner, a friend from the industry would come over and work with her on ideas. By that time, Assoulin had twenty years' worth of sketchbooks, though it took time to hone in on how all of her thoughts could translate into a real collection. "It took a lot of faith, and it was very daunting to suddenly create and bring everything into reality. It still feels like that every damn time. Our studio is safe and playful and creative and stressful, but it's like a womb—every time we have to put something out there you're frightened and you're never sure even if you've worked on it for two months or six months or twelve years."

What outweighed her discouragement and fear of failing was her hunger to outwork others in the industry. Though she didn't go to the perfect design school or have the pedigree that most think you need to become a good designer, her passion for creating almost burned a hole inside her because she cared that much. It wasn't until her second collection when her husband left his full-time job to help with the financials that investments and revenue starting locking into place. Assoulin credits his involvement as the missing piece to making the business function.

Assoulin spent a lot of time thinking about how her business would make a mark and be different from what was already in the market. Her experience from Oscar de la Renta and Lanvin gave her the tools to decipher what would help her business flourish in the beginning, and in the years following that. She had the experience of working with brands from the ground up to cultivate a vision for the brand beyond the first season. So when she started her own brand in 2012, she was able to grow fast. Rosie Assoulin is now sold in most major department stores, e-commerce sites, and D2C. It has received industry accolades along with regular red-carpet nods. Not to mention, her sales are incredibly strong. "I don't know how to say it perfectly but I just know that you always find a way. Whatever it is, if this thing doesn't work out, I think, 'Okay,' and have to prepare myself to find it because when you have something to say you have to be relentless."

People will pay $1,700 for a blouse from Assoulin because they know that it's made with the highest standards, it's beautiful, and it will provide the perfect amount of drama to any look—you can wear it with jeans and still look ready for the runway. All of the techniques and intricacies she learned from fashion houses are reflected in the nature of how pieces are made. There is a certain vibrancy and energy that only her clothes have. And in talking to her you can tell she loves so many things about the world and has the talent and creativity to take a curtain and make it look like a million bucks. But it's her curiosity to make things something that they would never have been, the urge to insert bright colors on silhouettes no one would ever consider, and experiment just enough to add an eclectic vibe to something so simple. Her line is a direct mirror of who is she and why she's been so successful. The clothes speak for themselves. They also sell themselves.

It also helps that Assoulin's vision is tightly focused. With the expansion of the brand in every season, you'll still see some of the same shapes but interpreted in new fabrics or silhouettes, in addition to some pieces that surprise you and some that take your breath away. You know what you're coming for, but it still brings you an unexpected joy that you don't often get from shopping anymore. Adjectives like *whimsical*, *easy*, and *voluminous* are reliable descriptors. "I like what happens when you take two pieces of fabric, or even just one piece, and play," she says. "I like the shapes, the story, the narrative, and anything that seems just unnecessarily fanciful." For Assoulin, the key to growing her collection season after season is that she is invested in the story each piece tells. She also always innovates and elevates. Something as simple as a blouse or trousers becomes much more because she takes in the whole picture, from the history of the fabric to the people she imagines who will wear the piece.

"I've seen how people become carnage in this industry," she notes. "There are so many talented people with visions, but I got this lucky because of all the people that put me up on their shoulders and generations that came before me." Especially as a female New York–based designer, there's a delicate balancing act, having this incredible opportunity to tell your story in a place that is so ripe with creativity, and realizing that being a designer now means so much more than creating clothing. "I struggle with the parts of the business that have nothing to do with the actual creation of clothing a hundred percent." She laughs. "Especially when it's your business and you're just trying to keep the lights on and keep the dream alive. Everybody that's working with you, with your customers and for yourself, because it's all running on your engine."

Innovation requires a constant balance of concerns. Assoulin doesn't use any animal skins or feathers, fur, or leather. She does, however, use responsibly sourced silk and wool (which aren't technically vegan) and recycled polyester. Finding a way to make pieces that are aesthetically adventurous and in line with her brand while also addressing the concerns of customers and maintaining best practices with production have been a challenge since Assoulin has to not only keep up with the times and culture but also service her own creativity. "If there is a disconnect between what you're putting out and you, you're going to burn out so quick it's going to kill you." Assoulin has found that it's no longer about focusing on sustainability, red-carpet attire, or a quota of a certain amount of looks per season. Instead she focuses on rejuvenating and contributing to culture and the environment. If you're making pieces for the sake of it or trying to produce something just for likes on Instagram, then your business is never going to work.

Remaining innovative, Assoulin is also constantly brainstorming about the future and advancements she can make with her brand as a whole. "I spend a lot of time thinking about how women are going to wear pieces and how you want them to perform. It's much more than what to wear to a dinner party; it's also that our clothing is going to have to perform for us the same way it did when we had to wear furs and skins to stay warm in the dark ages. I think about breathable fabrics and functionality because one day it's going to be too hot, and the environment is changing even now."

That thinking led her to create By Any Other Name, also known as BAON, which focuses on sleeker, more tailored silhouettes for workingwomen. It's basic in the best kind of way, and a smart business opportunity since most of her customers currently work in some creative field. BAON caters to people who work in serious corporate environments and need chic shirtdresses priced at just over $1,000. It's a smart move, as Rosie Assoulin the brand has exceeded its connection with customers. BAON feels like a natural extension of who Assoulin is at her core, instead of being a money ploy.

Assoulin operates with a staff of under twenty people in a modest SoHo studio. She has achieved an incredible amount at this size, but still has room to grow. Now with two different lines in play, Assoulin has also realized the importance of speed and competition in her growth. She has my trust as a designer I love. The fact that I can order one of her dresses on Net-A-Porter and get it the same day or, at the very latest, the next morning means something more than instant gratification. In a sea of endless options, keeping the customers who have helped you establish and build only continues if you can be the person they can count on time and time again.

Assoulin notes, "It never gets old to have the ability to take something that's an idea and bring it to life from sketch to muslin, that's always exciting." But on the other hand, the worst part can often be when you finally get a sample. "Honestly it's because your dream dies a bit—it's rarely better in person and lives up to expectations, so I spend a lot of time reassessing if it still works." That process alone is evident in Assoulin's clothing; there aren't any extras or leftovers, which makes for a very edited-down collection and helps cost and production fees.

The thought process that Assoulin takes herself through in creating every collection, down to what zippers to use, has allowed her to thrive in an oversaturated market. "It's so intense and probably too much, but I think about what do I want to put on my body and what do I want to see out there?" she says. "It's also about [what] I want to make but also what I think women would want someone to propose for them to wear that they would never pick out for themselves and be surprised by." Even though the collection is tightly edited, it hits on so many different emotional stages that you go through when getting dressed. Some days you want to disappear and not have to think about what you're wearing, and some days you're going to a meeting and want to be taken seriously—either way Assoulin has what you need.

"Some people might think our collection is a little schizophrenic because it amplifies different emotions, but for me it's a hundred percent authentic," she says. "I want to confront all the feelings people go through when getting dressed, and be there for them, and I think that's what made the brand flourish because how we dress in this moment, and the synthesis of what's happening in our lives is what's new under the sun."

At the end of the day, Assoulin attributes it all to bravery. "You don't want to be the person when you see their collection and it's nice but it doesn't feel truthful and honest to who they are. When you can tell that they're making pieces a certain way because they're at this house or that they're just making things for the sake of money . . ." She continues, "Putting yourself out there and accepting that people might not like it is hard. They might not like you. They might misunderstand you. But once you cross the hump of figuring out who you are and what you have to say to the world, everything is changed."

If you learn anything from reading about Rosie Assoulin, I hope that is to never give up figuring out your own way in this industry. Even if you have to have a million starts, you never know—that final start could catapult you into creating the brand you've always dreamed of. When people think of Assoulin, they think of sculptures and shapes that make a statement. But it's the fact that she turns the ordinary into something so exceptional, marvelous, and her own, that all anyone wants to do is be part of her world. There's nothing in her collection that doesn't feel special, and that you won't love decades from now.

5

LESSONS LEARNED

Looking back at the journeys of three designers from different backgrounds who have made it in fashion, there are countless lessons to learn. I think you realize by now that the path is no cakewalk. But it is filled with the purest sense of joy and love for making something out of nothing. And though I hope you've taken the time to read, study, and do your own homework and soul searching, here's the CliffsNotes summary of lessons I hope you never forget.

"STAY HUNGRY. STAY FOOLISH."

Yes, these are the famous words quoted by Steve Jobs in his 2005 commencement speech at Stanford University, but they apply to fashion people! You need curiosity, relentlessness, and a discerning eye to have something important to say. Attending a design school is up to you. That decision won't be a defining factor in your career if you're constantly exposing yourself to great design and studying the successes and failures of people who have come before you. Persevere through setbacks and failures. Failure is an opportunity to grow and learn. Keep your passion in the foreground but don't slip on the practical aspects of running a business.

TAKE IT SERIOUSLY

It seems like an obvious assumption that if you're reading this book, you're serious about becoming a designer. But until you're actually in the business, you have no idea. There are plenty of people who like fashion as a hobby, or maybe want to create something and sell it to their friends, but starting a business is an entirely different thing. Being a designer at a design house or for a mass-market company is different than creating a business plan, marketing it, generating revenue, and following through. If you strike out on your own, then you won't have the infrastructure and resources afforded to you by a large, established company. It's a competitive, saturated market rife with failure. Be prepared to take it seriously if you want to last.

SAY SOMETHING AND MEAN IT

As a young designer, it can be tempting to look at social media or go into a fast-fashion store and try to translate those trends into something you can make. Don't try to reinvent the wheel—you have to be who you are. Fall in love with other people's work, and don't be afraid to be influenced by others, but at the end of the day you need to be putting out something different and original. Differentiate yourself through your voice to cut through the noise. The things that break out are saying something new. In order to say something you have to know yourself, so dig deep and bring something authentic to the table. Create signature styles that play to your strengths, and your individuality will speak for itself. Be clear about who you are and where you want to go with your brand. Bridging the two will help you put the pieces of the puzzle of your brand and business together.

DON'T JOKE ABOUT YOUR MONEY

Depending on what you plan to create you'll need thousands of dollars, but designers have a bad reputation of lightly touching on the money subject in the beginning and then realizing that they don't have funds to create their dreams. I'm not saying that you have to be able to understand the intricacies of the stock exchange, but I am recommending that you have to learn about finances so that you know where your money is going. This all comes from building a solid groundwork and foundation as discussed in chapter one. Your business plan should be something you lose sleep over. It should be so foolproof that people cannot say no to your proposal. Decisions about money will either drive your business forward or drag it backward, leaving you to start all over again.

BE READY TO COMPROMISE

Ideally you shouldn't be doing this on your own. You'll need help, and asking for it is not a weakness. So be open to bringing someone onboard, preferably someone who strengthens your weaknesses. Be prepared to collaborate and match your vision to the realities of your plan. Be prepared to make creative sacrifices. Adjust and readjust. All your hopes and dreams and wishes will not be master-pieces, and some pieces just won't sell no matter how much you love them. Thinking that you "know it all" and there-fore people will follow you is foolish. Be prepared for your business partner or someone else on your team to have differing opinions about the direction of the brand. Be flexible enough to insert basics or more affordable pieces into your line to help with sales. It's all a balancing act, and if you are making more in sales, you can potentially use that money to cover expenses for avant-garde pieces. How much of you as an individual that goes into those pieces is completely your choice—but no matter what you'll have to balance making things in your own image with allowing others to see themselves in those pieces.

MISTAKES ARE EXPECTED— AS LONG AS YOU LEARN FROM THEM

I guarantee that even after you've read all this advice you'll still overspend on a collection because that's just the way creatives dream up things. I guarantee that any money you get, whether it be from your first small round of funding from family and friends or a big investment from a venture capital firm, you'll look back and wonder why you didn't spend more money on a certain item or why manufacturing costs drained your budget. There are going to be mistakes on this journey because there are a million little decisions every day to make in a hurry—but as long as you learn from wrong decisions and use them to build and grow your brand, that should give you a bit less anxiety.

IN THE END, IT is difficult to articulate the pains and joys of being a designer. The late and imitable photographer Bill Cunningham perhaps put it best, "Fashion is the armor to survive the reality of everyday life." And what a privilege it is to create that armor, to design dreams, to be part of culture.

ACKNOWLEDGMENTS

Look, Mom! I wrote a book! Thank you for always being my toughest editor. Thank you to my wonderful family—Andre, Dad, Mom, Dee, and Jerome—for all your support. Kisses to my sweet Jay and the most fashionable person I know, Harper Garrett. And thank you to my kind and wonderful husband, Andre—I truly do not know where I would be in this life without you.

REQUIRED READING

How to Slay: Inspiration from the Queens and Kings of Black Style by Constance White

Fashion: The Definitive History of Costume and Style by DK Smithsonian Museum

The Fairchild Dictionary of Fashion 3rd Edition by Charlotte Mankey Calasibetta

SCHOOLS TO CONSIDER

Accademia Costume & Moda, Roma Italy
Amsterdam Fashion Institute, Amsterdam, Netherlands
Central Saint Martins, London, United Kingdom
China Academy of Art, Hangzhou, Zhejiang, China
Design School Kolding, Kolding, Denmark
Drexel University, Philadelphia, United States
Fashion Institute of Technology, New York, United
    States
London College of Fashion, London, United Kingdom
Parsons School of Design, New York, United States
Savannah College of Art & Design, Savannah, Georgia,
    United States

ABOUT THE AUTHOR

Lindsay Peoples Wagner is the editor-in-chief of *Teen Vogue*. She has previously worked at *The Cut*, *New York* magazine, and Style.com. While at *The Cut*, she won the ASME Next award in 2017, honoring outstanding achievement by magazine journalists under the age of 30. More recently, Peoples Wagner wrote the critically acclaimed feature "Everywhere and Nowhere: What it's really like to be black and work in fashion," that showcased more than 100 people of color's insights and perspectives on diversity in fashion. Peoples Wagner, who hails from Wisconsin, graduated from Buena Vista University with a bachelor's degree in art and journalism. She currently resides in Brooklyn.